Sleepwalk into Eternity

Library of Congress Control number: 2024920582
ISBN: 9798991125024
Published by: Alegria Publishing
Book cover and layout by: @mckadamia

Sleepwalk into Eternity

Rosa Christina

ALEgRÍA PUBLISHING

To those friends and family
who always pull me back to earth.

CONTENTS

PREFACE

When I was young, I was convinced my house was haunted. Our living room walls were made of mirrors, set directly in front of a wide window, right down the hall from my room. In daylight, it was airy and open, spreading sunshine across peach walls and doubling the size of the room. As a child, it was a source of constant theorizing and fantasizing. I believed it to be an extension of my world, a closed off room I could never enter. I would imagine characters from my father's bedtime stories living somewhere in the "other" living room. My mother and I would sit in front of glass walls and would host puppet shows in front of them, my dolls acting as the audience to their own performance. And sometimes, I would sit alone where mirrored edges intersected and poured into each other endlessly, and marvel that I could keep myself company.

It was different at night. I would peer through my door at reflections of streetlights making their way through the window's glass and to my bed. As it got darker, and curtains were drawn, and hall lights were dimmed, I would instead look at reflections of shadows, lost in a static of darkness, flickering and shifting as I tried to make out their shape and failed. Their amorphous and ephemeral nature made those shadows all the more monstrous to my five-year-old eyes. For a long while, I couldn't sleep. I spent much of my time vigilantly staring out of my bed and into my living room, ensuring that the entities stayed where they always stood; in the creases of yellowed curtains, nearly blackened through dim streams of moonlight. Gradually, daylight brought me less and less comfort, as their absence only raised more questions in my mind. Did they dissipate in the light, like any other shadow? Or were they simply hiding, watching me from spaces I couldn't see? Conversations with my parents registered as transient and echoed, secondary to racing calculations in my mind. If my eyes strayed away from my mother, and caught sight of a mirror, would I see them there too? I was so sure I would. Even as I spent time in the garden with my grandmother, the dirt beneath my fingers seemed less corporeal than the possibility of strangers hidden in the foliage.

My fear made these things real, even if no one else saw them, and it paralyzed me. All I could do was stay vigilant. I studied them; I noted that these shadow people never seemed to leave their 3am liminal habitat. I crafted a narrative around them; they were phantasmic residuals of a previous family. A nebulous pair, perhaps a brother and sister, or a husband and wife, or a parent and child. Safe actors in a safe story…so long as they stayed in the mirror and I stayed in my room.

Detach, observe, rearrange. A simple ritual burned straight into the lizard brain.

I'm hardly the first or only child who has memories like these; of beings emerging from the dark, limbs arranged into the vague outline of a man, leering at their petrified audience. There are many accounts of shadow people; from collective childhood memories of the hat-man, to the red-eyed terror of sleep paralysis. Perhaps the most famous accounts are those of Los Vigilantes Oscuros, or "the dark watchers", entities lingering upon the horizon of the Santa Lucia Mountains in California that can be observed at a distance, but disappear beneath scrutiny. Some say these beings are manifestations of negative energy– drawn to our extraordinary tangles of anger and anxiety and fear. Others believe they are interdimensional silhouettes, imprints from another world left upon the veil of space and time. Or perhaps, these entities are not beings at all. Perhaps they are simply memories, echoes released from the earth like smoke from a fire.

There is nothing quite as human as ascribing meaning or shape where there is none. And there is nothing quite as human as ascribing moments of uncertainty a supernatural kind of significance. The variance of the shadow people and their stories is emblematic of this and the vagueness of what they are and what they want gives the right dosage of dread and plausibility. It's the lure of the unknown, but gift-wrapped in tourist trappings; a mystery given a human shape, but without the means, or incentive, to investigate its purpose. Everyone has felt a bit of fear in the dark. Contextualizing it within the confines of mythology gives that fear a removed sense of purpose. They're like horror movies in that way– terror transformed into a spectacle, and ourselves into mere spectators. Shadows in a mirror, separate and fading.

In my case, my connection with these creatures was a harbinger of the kind of relationship I would have with my own mind. As I grew older, I still looked in corners for silent watchers. Shadows shifted, from amorphous shapes into malevolent entities with malicious intent. My thoughts began to take new lives of their own, gorged on external variables of religious paranoia until they were just as autonomous as I was. Sometimes it seemed they had far more power than I did. They certainly felt more real than I did; there was a certainty to their constant presence that superseded my ability to perceive my day to day as more than a dream. And so, I took up the ritual born from my childhood. I pushed the shadows into the glass walls of my mind, and kept vigil. They stayed in the living room, and I stayed in my room. I made them villains within the self-sustaining mythology of my fear.

To be clear, there is a functionality to separation. There is no use in letting fears, unfounded or otherwise, eat you from the inside out. I myself was often told that the best thing I could do with my fear —and later, my OCD– was to see it as a separate entity; a thing not born of you that invaded your mind. And to be clear, this does help…when the point of this sort of contextualization is management. When the goal is to grant you autonomy over the terror. But there is a temptation, I think, to do the opposite; to grant these entities control while we become mere observers within our own minds. We ourselves become those dark watchers, overlooking the landscape of our lives.

And as with all things, there is no experience that is truly internal. We live in a time and place that encourages, each and every one of us, to be voyeurs. We have developed our own rituals of distance, relegating ourselves to a perpetual state of audience. Our world deems us incorporeal within our own realities; we linger at the peripherals of our own experiences, and only exist in the moments that we are observed. I feel at times we operate as though we have decided to live in mirrored realities, as shadow people that dissipate at any meaningful interaction.

We isolate ourselves within our own minds and call it healing. We look toward a procession of visages; aesthetics of another time, love stories from afar, the comfort of religion, to give us shape. We convince ourselves that rituals of detachment are journeys of self-realization. But while we have given ourselves the role of spectator of stories around us, we can never fully separate ourselves from being actors. We use our experiences to shape our world, to shape our fears, no matter how still we stand.

When I think on the shadow people from my childhood, what I try to remember is not the shadows themselves, but the moments they stole, yet gave them shape. My mother telling me stories of love transcending eternity. My father working long hours but still having time to crack a joke. My grandmother singing praises to God while working in the garden. It was acts of love that softened my horror, changed the shape of my fear into comfort.

Much of my writing has been attempts to capture rituals of paranoia and anxiety that have long been staples of my life, and transform them into opaque pieces of imagery. But most of all, this collection of poems, with its little stories and strange characters, are my personal call to action, a journey incomplete, shared with the world. I hope these poems are at least a start to recognizing the rituals of separation you create within your own life.

Fight the rot, and break the ritual.

A Requiem of a Meeting

I

Night begun
and so did we.

No stars lit the path
we walked, with sisters
cold and dark
hiding
suns from courtships
of dawn.

No knight breached the walls
we built, save twins
old and sad
guiding
breath from towers
long red.

I counted
bones in my wrist
I traced
lines in my palms
I thought
I could sleepwalk
forever.

II

Night fell,
and so did you.

Black water stained the sky
and clung to the names carried
along banks of pulsing rivers
flooding forgotten temples and
crowning bone basins with a howl.

A thousand pebbles danced
across the slick of your eyes
and stirred foggy tears trailing down
scraped skin.

Air carved a door in your throat
and ran down the steps in your neck
until you choked on the footsteps
it left behind.

Dead white knuckles grasped
damp wheat grass,
feet dangled over
night's black maw.

You dug yourself deep
so you wouldn't
fall in.

III

Night faded,
and so did I.

I woke up one evening and felt
Metaphysical dust bunnies scamper
through my eye's tunnel.
I pressed slippery, iridescent tracks
upon sclera moonscapes,
and through the snow
of black static
I found the echo
of a Shape
riding orange streetlights
through stained apartment windows
to visit an old flame
flickering in my neighbor's attic.
I tapped my finger against the glass,
and cut myself on a look
broken by the blade
of a sharp gaze
and fell
into pieces
of you.

IV

We chased sunlight
into the woods.

You flitted through soft green prisons
and jumped through sun-made stars
and tumbled through bark-made night.

I watched
through curtains of wilted leaves
dripping the scent of death upon
newly sprung flowers,
the stench peeled the sight from your eyes

until you were left with nothing
but the feeling of
an idea of
an image of
me.

V

This is the story
of how we met.

I loved you
from afar

and

you loved me
from a dream.

in the dark

Hymn of Crafts

Strangers knock an empty song
Peddling doom, such good news.
They offer words, warm as milk,
Within dark scrolls of honey;
Sweet-stained upon your lips,
Rot curdled on your tongue.

Out there be monsters,
Beyond your horizon
Blank and black, living lands;
Hungered jaws, dripping stars
Calling for the taste of awe.

Out there be monsters
Strangers of light, smiting eyes
Pouring white in elder dawns;
Pink skies and blackened wounds
Bleeding out the years of you.

Be not afraid, say the lost
Walk within your open wound
Split weeping by the crescent moon
Longing sweetly for the day.
Listen for the howl and haunt
Of spirits searching for their shape.

Inertia

We, lost souls, blow out the torch
And gouge our eyes from traveled paths
And cut our tongues on winded thoughts
And dream instead a drowning shore.

We, lost souls, abandon sail
And break our limbs to fill our lungs
With heavy tastes of fearful lust
That bind our breath with dread and dust.

We, lost souls, hunt for our graves
We dig in secret, and dig alone
Damning doors in lore and dusk
But at shame's door, the sun still knocks.

For the sea does not take out of hunger;
The sky does not thirst for our fear.

The Fisher Kings

Beneath giants, they scuttle
Old gods, traveling wastes.
Glinting armour, hiding wings
Cursed with immortality.

This world was built too big
For little truths, leaving
Lifetimes lost in the vast
Beginnings and ends.

Old things are to be forgotten
Or so we wish, as victors
Write triumphs in the dark
For the young to read.

They travel still, ugly and ancient
They spread their wings and rise.
Dark angels, with their testaments.
O gods, the beginning and the end.

Gravity

Theirs was a language of looks
Secrets suspended upon the want
Of a Spider.

Thin tangles weighed by the long sighs
Of gods, dismantling leers
So sheer in gauze, a threaded
pause.

Theirs was a language of looks
strange tongues in promised lands
Gentle guide, so sly
lending eyes that bind
Longing, drawn near,
I Fear.
They wades woven ponds
shrouded in shadow.

Theirs was a language of looks
But ours is a Howl, windswept
Earth and sea, a push and pull–
You to me.
Primal phantoms yawn their chasms
In silence, and walk the walls
Of my kiss, of my arms.

There is no language to learn.
Burn.

Spectre

I found the bits of him scattered
In the fields without soil or sun.
In the days that rained nights,
Did he plant his delights--
The spectre that bloomed in the dark.

Dust stole my breath with his wind
And froze in the frost of my lungs.
And rose from the graves
That carried no names
My spectre that bloomed in the dark.

Journey did I barren wastelands,
In gorges that swallowed the sun.
But tomb nor bone
Nor wood nor stone
Housed he who bloomed in the dark.

I spoke smoke into silence,
A secret forged ancient and new.
A call for the soul
Who wandered alone
A spectre who bloomed from the dark.

From wombs of death bloomed my spectre,
A ghost born of dreams and the hope
Of futures well-traveled
And my fears unraveled
In echoes he bloomed with the dark.

I search for water

I search for water
In a dark and frozen lake.
Its glass reflects my longings
Before my thoughts take shape.
But beneath the streams
Of coin and currency
I taste only wine;
A dry and bitter drink.

I search for water
In the halls of ancient wars
Remade, reforged, transformed
Into postcards to send home.
I look for answers
In legends I uphold.
But still my mind remains
In that dark and frozen lake.

I search for water
In a forest, vast and black.
I can only go there
Through threaded thoughts of paths.
I search temporal deserts
Pass through a spatial gash
But still there is no quenching
The darkness in my hands.

Hymn of Acts

A stranger sounds his horn
Yearning laced within the howl
Sealed in vows, a breathing gash
Panting blood with airless gasps
Scratching sounds as it drowns
All at once, then not at all.

A stranger bares his blade
A gleaming grin, a crescent moon
Scarring night with bleeding light.
He haunts your woods, a starving god
Crawling back, through bony glass,
Begging burial in your heart.

Be not afraid, they sing on high
Starved we are, but stay for you
We hunger for your gentle gaze
Blind and wide, Faithful and kind;
Cuts flayed open into eyes.

in the walls

Three

There are three things that make a home
The wood, the bed, the open stove.
I stop by, every now and then
To sleep beneath the dark and din.

There are three things that make a road
The earth, the sky, the map unknown
I travel here, now and then
And find the graves of gods and men.

There are three things that make a soul
A want, a will, a memory
I find mine, every now and then
I close my eyes, forget again.

The Wanderer

I like to walk in the forest
Beneath eyes, blackened burls;
Upon earth, disturbed and turned;
My steps, a crushing memory
Engraved in morning dew.

I like to wander the valleys
Chatter with souls, old and grim
Bend their backs and howl their hymns
Pull my roots and climb their limbs–
A wreckage of Creation.

I like to hide in the woods
Seek those giants, cloaked in grey.
Fragile legs, waking and wading
Dreary days, praying and praising
Spalted seconds within a heart.

I stand in congress
Bone white splinters
Rising beneath rock,
Below the prism of air
And sky.

I'll find you in the green chapel
Gift you ascension, rooted firm
Beneath eyes, soft and warm
Upon earth, tossed and turned.

The Traveler

I saw a man in the woods
Who watched me as I walked
He cruised by me, a neutral grin
Cloaked beneath a pungent mist
Lit by the wick of a cigarette.

Eyes wide and white,
Slipped between trees
Peeling birch, here to there.
Limbs split to lips, red leaves
Spilling down to crowds
Of a thousand, dark words
Marching spirals, starved and vile
Within his stream of speak.

I fled to a house in the distance
Collapsed under the weight
Of bright lights and black skies
Brown boots and red dye
Loose boards, hollow floors.

Eyes sick and pale
Pressed upon the glass.
Inverse shade, painting light
Falling neatly across the grass.
It cut thick through mist and smoke,
This man, I think, he shifts and bloats,
Stretching leathered and weathered skin;
His youth, an ill-tailored fit.

I hid my trail, godly and good
And set my sights to yellow stars.
I followed wisps, faint and dark–
A scent of he who found my face
Within the shape of wilting moss.

Eyes wet and ripe
Rolled down hillsides;
Ephemeral boulders
Bruised my shoulders
As I knocked at his door.
I rattled locks, red with rust,
I prowled his panes, a sickly pawn
Waiting for the rising sun.

I saw a man in the woods
Who tried to take me home.
He hid away weakly
Within walls he built me
But patience is the virtue of two.

The Guest

Once, you may have found the woods comforting, a cocoon of bark and leaf insulating the most raw and primal parts of you. Tonight, all you hear is the whistling of wind, winding through gnarled limbs and brittle wood, and all you feel is the cold sludge of blood, smeared black upon your palms.

Behind you, the house grows no less small with distance. The stone lodge, so kitschy and and carefully eerie by daylight, has lost all whimsy in the dim starlight. Dark windows look down upon you, and you think you see something flicker beneath their blank, glassy stare. It sees you as you are, knows that you have witnessed its work. And now, it witnesses mine, you think.

You wonder, as your footprints melt into snow, deepened with the weight of your secret.

The Lover

His limbs are made of tangled lines,
A slip of white in dead of night
A pallid face, carved and cold
A crescent moon, dark and low.

He gifts me pictures, pretty things
Dripping paint on blackened sheets
Vivid greens, angry blues
'A gift of dreams, from me to you.'

I love his fingers, bony white
They draw me places out of sight
I love his kisses, hot and thin
They tear my thoughts from where I've been.

He swallows flames that burn the cold
To keep me safe, in hall and home.
He hangs his cloak upon the glass
So my bones won't feed the grass.

His smile fades with morning light
But still I wait, and stay inside.
In his arms, my walls are warmed
In his arms, I am alone.

The Name

My lover sleeps within my heart
And hangs his pictures on my walls.
He builds me towers, stony woods
Lighting nerves on empty paths.
He cloaks me with his frigid skin,
Warms my throat with scalding lips.

We walk along a sprawling shore
Beneath the bloom of greying trees
He holds my hand, I grasp his wrist
What is your name, I mean to ask,
But lose my voice to a kiss.

There, he says, across the way
Beyond the mud, beyond the lakes
Within the cities I have left
Inside the house I have built
Beneath the bed I once slept
Hide the words I cannot say.

Find the fissure in the floor
Break the boards, claw the cracks
Scrape the dirt, wet and red
Gouge the gorge I left behind
A space I saved for you and I.
In the dirt beneath your skin
There lies the name I cast away.

The Heir

Floorboards creak and carry
the ghost of his weight
Walls sigh with the sound
of his secrets.
I wake in the night, pried
Open by plaster, and fed
Fractal shards of thoughts
Born of a heart not mine.
Shadows dipped in earth
Run their hands across
My brow, and leave me
With thoughts of you.

This house was not built for me
Still I sleep, and I sleep well
In barren rooms, left alone,
I dream a love not my own.

Therefore

I think
someone let the night inside
my house to drink
the blue light from my eyes
and tuck clarity
into a nest of needles
shifting in sand sheets
beneath the cold
of my fingertips and
I think
my eye itches with grains
of thought that roll
across white deserts
and chase colors
out the door and
i think
i want to follow

but black cats
eat lights like rats
and the dark melts
wet and warm
into my skin
and i swim deep
with the fish in my blood and
in the creeks in my ribs
and i
can hardly
think
of the dawn
and the dusk
and the dark
and the green
that sing celestial silence
and i hope
they eat the meal of me
and take with them
the sound of this
strange music.

Thereafter

Hear there the clawing grey
that mettles wood
and scrapes the grain to find
the pain that beats within
the heart that peels
against the sharpened rib
and falls apart deep within
fissured fractures forming fractals
upon the pattern
upon the wood
upon the splinters
digging deep beneath
the iron and
the flesh and
the popping strands of skin
that parts the reddened sea
and finds there the
fear that scrapes the grain to find
the pain that whispers
plain beyond the pulp
and through the pores
and beats
an empty pulse
an empty place
a sky that falls apart
upon the want
of a nail.

You should turn your lights off
before you go to sleep

I woke up in the middle of the night, my eyes dry beneath fluorescent lights. The plastic clock on the wall said it was 2am, but the walls were washed with a bright shine, a ravenous artifice dulled by yellowed paint. My mind too came alight with thoughts of dawn, though my bones were dark with sleep, and my neck, still as stone, forced my sight towards a single, flickering bulb. Wasted energy. The bill's going to be crazy, I told myself, though I could not recognize the spider's web peeking from my peripheral, and though the sheets scratching my skin were a strange strain of cotton.

I need to turn off the lights, I thought, and watched as shapeless luminescence stretched into limbs branching down towards my brow. The blinding white dimmed into a silver moon, dancing beneath the lids of my eyes and leaving phantom stains in my head. Somewhere there, between the unfamiliar brightness and the lulling call of sleep, I traced the outline of a mouth. It hummed across the dark cracks of the ceiling, and slid down the bare walls of this home. It sang to me, black lips floating in my head, low notes quivering its music beneath my skin.

A thread floated from the forgotten web. It flickered towards this room's only sun, and for a moment it glittered, a shining strand of gold. What a waste, I thought, and watched the light fade 'til I fell back to better dreams.

Idolatry of the heart

Bury your image within me, o love.
Chase the echo of your presence
Across the gap in my chest.

I deny the sepulcher
And make instead a bed of boats.
I tend to children
Buzzing, crawling, searching
Bony basins, whetting pain
Cradled within my womb.

You have made me an effigy of
Beauty, but I have swallowed
The last vestiges of mortality.
I am the patron saint of the swarm
Floating in rivers of milk and honey.

If you worship me, find my altar
In the grime of your sink
In the crumbs on your plate
In the blue light
Of your television.

in the garden

Atlas

I saw an ant
carry the weight of a leaf
little, lost and alone.
I plucked away her burden
and left her to wander
her empty lot.

Angels in the garden

Upon the road to hearth and home
Stands a pillar, ever still,
It wears a veil, staining red,
In pools of blue and brown and gloom
Built beneath those woods I roamed
With friendly fire, long ago.

Today it wades in lakes of leaves
Draped in earth left behind
Ornate eyes gazing on high
Raising hands, long ghost and gone,
Weighed with blades of grass and rock;
A graven mirror in a grove.

A quiet wind carries a thought
Wisps of words from far away
A quiet wind carries a change
And gently wipes its face away.

Lady of the Lake

We went to the lake in the middle of May, and
watched the bend of air push back the mirror we
called ice.

I put on my skates and my coat, and
he told me it was the middle of May
but I skated between the
thin line carved in
thawing
Fear.

He said you're playing a Dangerous Game
I told him Games were the only things
I knew how to play, and he said it was
the middle of May, and I laughed at him
as the Lady cracked her Window open.
(just for me).

His arms,
thin and
pale and
Lovely.

I fell,
tears
softly
melting
May flowers.

I think I'll try to call this air,

and Breathe.
I've been drowning for so long,
I fall in love with anyone
who thinks I'm
Swimming.

The Jeweled Prince

My tongue is still
My lips are bare
I taste the earth
I slumber there.

My mother weeps through the stone
My father, through the trees,
But my lover travels still
To kiss the scent upon my teeth.

My Prince rides on wings of silk
Pale in sight, cloaked in black
Cold hands upon my ruins
Jeweled eyes upon my skin.

He seeks in me forgotten paths
And phantom temples hidden there
In my walls, he finds a home
A little life in ancient lands.

Travel down my stony steps
My muted beauty, sickly sweet
White walls rise, still lakes lie
He comes to pray, my Prince of Peace.

I lost my voice to the wind
My echoes scatter, faint and sharp
My lover finds them, in his faith--
Water gathered in a wound.

My love is made for silent halls
Still he hums a secret song.
His eyes cut a thousand ways
And bleeds a gaze sweet and gone.

Adam's Sermon

I search for Christ in you
I cradle welts in my palms
Forged with sweat, though
I prefer to think I am anointed
By tides of dust left behind.

I search for Paul in me
Sun beating down on my brow
As you dig through the light
In my eyes, and paint my skies
Bright with your signs.

I sanctify the lie
In symbols of tradition,
In rhythmic palpitation.
Breathe deep in earth,
Eyes glazed with dirt
Inhale your prayer and
Count the seeds
Gathered in your lungs;
I will rise again.

In light of sky's perdition
In spill of blood's ambition
Roots run down, run deep
Growing chapels
Never seen.
Speaking sermons
Lost in me.

This time, you have made me
From the prettiest dead things.
Scattered souls saved,
And renamed
Into your ritual.

Poseidon Dating in LA

I live for flow of conversation,
streams running cold
towards destinations
desired and denied.
We arrive to crossings
calm and still, yet
waves flood
my ribs and I lose
my mind to rapids
cooling stone beneath
my skin.

It's cold and alone in the current
state of things. I see his ship,
blue sails glittering with flames
smearing skies with smoke screens
until red dawns run our lips dry.

Whispers flow freely
through parched wood,
slaking thirst born
from lakes of fire
begging me
for shelter and shores
But no bridges.

Captain of one,
warm and soft
collecting salt
unfurling tangles
I cannot unravel
by teeth alone.

Upon dawn, I wake and see
the imprint of his absence
and I like him so much more
Now that he's gone.

night swim at a lake

We love the chance for depth,
Dive in glass, breaking pace
Cracking pane, liquid shards
Pulsing rhythm, thrumming walls
The song of blood, calling sharks.

I think I long for languid lakes
A mountain looming over shores
A promise casting shade and stone
Upon a mirror I call my own.

As above, so below,
The sky I claim, clear as day
I swim therein, with my thoughts
Safely sank, safely changed.

It swims with me, my elder love
It climbs inside, a whispered leer
Peering in with kingly eyes
Hollow maws I fall inside.

I do not swim near stagnant shores
Nor look for comfort in the shade
Still I fear, I lent an ear
And left it bleeding in the waves.

Dracula

I sleep on my bench
Throat parched in
Cold drought.
Concrete red and wet
with reigns of terror
churning storms
upon my roof.

I build a house on
unhallowed ground.
the weight of day
drains freely into
riverbeds wrung
dry of
Sunlight.

I love her
the way stone
carries copper
scents storing
rainwater memory
buried beneath
scorched earth.

I love her and
riverbeds
dream of
Seas.

Reaper's Girl

In barren hills I passed today,
He grew me fields of flowers

He cut his foot on burning stone
To quench the scorch of thirsting earth
He plucked his scars and pruned his bones
To shining pillars, gleaming white.

His hands smelt ore to steel,
Cooked devils burning smoke and ash.
His hands smelled of grass and earth,
Tender skin with scents of rain.

He hoped the sun that scarred his skin
Would bleach these bones to flowers
But fires that burnt the heavens
Cooled to embers upon his tongue.

His eyes unraveled a river,
Slipping low and slow and narrow,
Spooling springs of tangled sound
Around his hills, around his heart;
A rope of tears he called a sea.

In barren hills, I passed today
And grew him fields of flowers.

Plenty of Fish

Fishermen throw their hooks,
Knitting nets with hymns
Thin and high-strung notes
Wading black water and
Swimming crystal seas.
Fish have fled these shores, but
Something swims beneath their boats
Flashing teeth beneath the waves.

Hunt the beast within the depths
And love the ache you set aside
Ancient sorrows swim
Across your lips, and flutter
Upon a bawdy chuckle--
Terror tastes so sweet in a song;
A copper taste in seas of salt.

You sail down my cheeks
Traveling to salted pools
Curdling damp static
Rolling over the soil
Of my tongue and
The stone of my teeth.

Hymn nor hook
Pierced its skin.
Still the beast sinks
Beneath the weight
Of tangled threads.

in the city

City of Sleep

Here lies death, feeble and sleeping in houses that feed him
mementos
Scraped from glass bowels left vacant and homeless in
hearts once kin.
Lord of the dark and the green now grey, faded and hungry
and begging
Paupers and wisemen for comfort, for prayer, for
knee and throne.

Another year passes roaming alone in a city
of sleep where
Death left me waiting in weddings of earth and of
sea and sky.
Wanders now he under bridges that moan for the meal that
he promised
Me in my dreams on his knees with his heart and his
hearth laid bare.

I once believed him a garden of stories, of fallen
seeds planted
Deep in my bags full of cats til they bloomed into
tender beasts.
Now I believe that the only thing gifted to me by
the green is
Forests of wood growing me and my heart into
hollowed halls.

Now and again, I am offered the scraps of a stranger
who tasted
Home in the words only heard from those lonely and
wedded ghosts.
Still and unmoving and waiting for eyes to behold a
strange love, he
Scraped from mementos left vacant and homeless in
hearts once kin.

.

Round One

'Hey!'
The howl of drink is a greeting
Even as I sit alone at a bar
And warm myself with the taste
Of temporary delusion.

I do not think to look
At the man who wears a Nirvana shirt
Priced up into Vogue from the dollar bin.
'Hey,' he says, and he taps me
With soft hands, bent and bruised.

His card is as black as a forest
As he slides it down sticky linoleum.
He cuts through the haze of grime
With a grin. His teeth, wide and white,
His eyes, pearls before swine.

'I saw your shape in the window,
When you decided to cross over.'
He thinks he's being charming, but—
'That's creepy,' I tell him, and he laughs
As though my privacy is a joke.

He takes a shot, amber liquid
Drips down his lips, like rain in a cave.
'I was lost 'til yesterday,' he tells me.
'When I finally came out of the forest
And I finally slipped out of the dark.'

I think on the trees that line town's edge
With bony branches and blood-brown leaves.
It's the kind of place tourists love,
With legends you take to the campfire
While the ghosts stay here, alone.

His mouth coils up like a snail, a smirk
Sticky enough to catch the questions
I know he wants me to ask. I smile.
'I hope you found what you came for
Now that you're back with the living.'

He taps his fingers upon his cheek,
Worn limestone beneath a stream.
'I'm only here for the evening,
But I want to make it count
If you'll just hear me out?'

I looked at his drink and his card.
There's designer holes in his designer jeans.
'I've never seen a ghost buy a round.'
He laughs and says he'll buy me a drink,
But I won't touch what I can't see.

I can smell the liquor in his breath
And scent the mold upon his neck.
He pushes back his close-cropped hair
And shares a smile almost as sweet
As the cocktails sloshed across the bar.

'There is treasure to be found
If you can find the place
In the water, in the ground
Where I thought I'd find myself
In the woods outside of town.'

He drums his nails upon his glass
And waits for me to take the call.
But all I can say is what I know:
'Tourists often think
Getting lost is getting out.'

Round Two

There's a kind of showmanship
That clings to honest conversation
At 7PM on a Tuesday evening.
I just want to drift away, but
He clings to his cave like a root.

He taps his fingers against his glass
It echoes faintly, like drops in pools.
His smile curls down and I can see
Whitened teeth hugging the crease
Of purpled gums and cracking lips.

'You think I'm just passing through
But I'm here for peace and solitude.
Help me find my path anew
In the water, in the ground.
In the woods outside of town.'

I watch him tangle his hand
Through a fifteen-dollar haircut
He probably got on his lunchbreak
On his way past the bull. I say,
'I don't know you.'

He stares at stagnant whiskey.
'I'm just a shadow of a man
Within the mar of heated dreams.
Dried water, staining sand
Until it rises to meet the sun.'

I think he's more like dried vodka
Staining a grimy bathroom, but I listen
As he fiddles with his old new shirt.
'Water that gathers in the dark,' I say,
'Will find other things to feed.'

He spreads his fingers and shrugs.
'I searched for sense in the sediment,
And for sense in the sentiment.
Gradients of years gone by
Inscribed in ides of drought.'

He slips his card into his jeans,
Though I note, there are no pockets.
He turns to me again, brows furrowed
With some kind of shame that I
Cannot recognize.

'I saw you once, across the way,
The night I decided to chase the shape
Of spirits I couldn't pour down my throat.
I sometimes wonder, would I have stayed
Had I stopped and said, 'hello'?'

Round Three

He leans towards me, and runs his thumbs
Across the foggy edge of a shot glass.
'In the woods, I thought I'd find
A promised place for me to wake
Deep beneath the rock and stone—'

'But you found yourself alone.'
Low lights dance along dark walls
As I stare into a half-empty bottle.
His fingers twitch and inch towards mine,
This man that smells of petrichor.

'I am less than what I was
When I saw you in the sepulcher.
I've made myself from watered clay
From blackened pools that I did wade
Beneath the woods outside of town.

'I wandered in tunnels cold and dark
And quenched my thirst in sunless creeks.
But in that time, I only dreamed
Of sitting down to share a drink
With the girl I saw across the street.'

He smiles at me, soft and sad,
And gently takes my hand in his.
'Help me find the rest of me
In the water, in the ground
In the woods outside of town.'

I pull away, and tell him straight—
'I don't know where you are
In the woods outside of town.
And you don't know who I am;
We're strangers talking in a bar.'

The man shifts in his ironed shirt
Scarred with wrinkles absent from skin.
I take a sip from my glass,
A drink I bought myself
Half a century before.

'I don't know you,' I say again.
His eyes shine, doeful and hurt,
And I hate how soft he looks beneath
The harsh veil of green bar lights.
So I say, 'Next round is on me.'

I turn to give him a drink,
And watch the glass pass his hands
Pretty and pale, translucent flesh
That sifts like smoke beneath my touch
And fades until I'm alone again.

I spill the whiskey upon the floor
As its taste burns into my throat.
It darkens, dries, and stays;
More water on the ground
In these woods outside of town.

Idealization of Heaven and Earth

Upon our hill, I dream of this:
Knotted hair of golden webs;
Visors of glass, gleaming black
Riding thunder, roaring mists
Hung low upon dark armour
That smells of leather.

We sit watching city lights
Glass eyes blooming cracks
Of perception, a prism of petals
Casting glows into the night.
Their gaze travel the miles
And claw your stony face,
Cutting rivers down your neck;
A web of shade in starry strands.

You like watching
Life lurking in the lines
Binding imprints of light.
Breath stirring beneath brick,
Steps thrumming steady rhythms
Carrying echoes of giants;
Monuments of possibility we built
For your soul's salvation.

I like watching
Grass beneath our hands.
Your arms, warm and far;
Dew drops, cold and here.
Sharp roots holding down
Broken blades bent and left
Engraved with meetings past.

I like watching
Your wilting mouth.
A smile ebbing waves
Upon my cheek, past my neck
Down to your planted city;
Offering approximations
Of affection.

Upon our hill, I dream of this,
A pool of mist, a beast of bone
Glinting silver, riding steel.
It prowls, four legs, two backs
Eyes searching the heavens.
Eyes leaving the heart.

City Without Streets

This city has no streets,
No alley shades, no lanes.
Only walls, raised up high
Gleaming glass, cheap lights
Spaces stacked on vacant heights;
A glinting quilt of metal.

These houses have no rooms
No kitchens and no beds
Only skin, pale and thin
Airy eyes, mechanized.
Papers stacked outside a door
No one opens anymore.

I peel away layers of concrete,
Stand my ground sinking down
Cascades of sand, sidewalk scars
Scabbed with hearts and names.
Earth remains, wet and red
Black blood and cold mud.

Dig deep beneath
Tiled threads of halls
Woven walls and empty malls
Pulsing clay, made bare
Shriveled roots, unaware.

This city has no streets
No paths for you to find
Nothing left to tread
Nowhere left to hide.

A Waiting Room

There is a room, clean and neat
It still smells of a pipe, freshly puffed.
A pair of shoes, worn and loved,
Remain tucked beneath a bare bed;
Treasures left for her purview.

Cleanliness is a pungent scent
That fills the mind with cluttered
Panic, a vile and unnatural lack
Inviting strangers to plant their lawns
In the desert of uncertainty.

Air thins and cools, and she wonders
If she should be alone for this long.
A hand passes, and then another
One gives time, one gives truth.
They are not meant for each other.

The Meek

A hundred years befall in storms,
Heavy rain a hungered swarm
Gnawing wet on brick and stone
To search for light from long ago.

A hundred years feeds the fields
Flooding streets to muddy streams
That rush thruways and seep in walls
Of empty stores with empty dolls.

Now comes the new, little roots
A cloak of green upon the beams.
Now come the old, sprouting spores,
A realm of gods upon a dream.

in a dream

The Sun King And His Ghost of Light

Once a prince, he lived in dreams
Of dancing maids and kissing kings.
But woke alone to barren lands
And bent his knee to a stench
That lingered still, stale and sweet.

Eyes find echoes, as do ears,
Vibrant voices, spooling shades
Of darkened paint, illustrious calls
Across the miles, across the years;
She called his name, his ghost of light.

He traveled then, across the plains,
Those empty lands that knew his name,
Through gleaning ruins, barren white,
He sheltered there, beyond a door
That stood alone, without a home.

She flew to him, his ghost of light,
A stain of shadow in the sky
Draining down her silver eye.
She wove her gaze, in shining strands,
A gauze of dark across his face.

She whispered water, gentle waves
Beyond a lake of blackened space.
How cool her call, a honeyed balm,
That cracked the ice of stagnant songs
And washed away the smell of rot.

He stayed with her, beyond the door
Above the crack of broken earth
Beneath the shell of open sky
They joined in words, they joined in minds
They joined in empty paradise.

He liked the way her shadows moved
And danced a veil upon her skin.
He loved the moonlight's molten lines
That filled her shape and left him blind
With muted magic of the night.

But suns do rise, a blazing noose,
A thread of days weaving weeks
Of mild moments, a churning slew.
Daylight spread its vile pools
Damp and thin, mundane and true.

She drank the poison of the dawn,
Time ate away her faded face
Left it blank, then filled its shape
With bugs and creatures, squirming things
That found in her a place to sleep.

Her curtains lift, rolls of skin
Hiding mirrors, gleaming white
Windows rise, a yellowed glass
Pretty prison parched with thirst,
Damp with little drops of light.

Now, the sun king builds his temple
With hungered stone, forged from lack
Dried mud flaking, soil staining
Walls of ivory, a fort of silence
Built beneath cracking lips.

He calls to her, his ghost of light
Who left her home in the night
To be with one who cannot hear
Her voiceless lips as they call,
I am changed, but I am loved.

Dark Watcher

I see your form, dark sister
Through mar of window panes,
Faded ink upon yellowed pages
Seeking power from the sun.

This earth is cold, your step is soft
You follow me, shade to shape
Out of sight, a flame of black
Shining low in light of day.

Hide in your hills, sweet sister.
And damn your rivers into wells.
Shadows dry and die by sunrise
But leave their mark in me.

This is Grief

A CERTAIN MAN awoke in a forest
and asked rivers to cleanse the rot
that grew beneath his nails,
and asked the earth to devour the sun
he buried in secret each season.
But he remembered, and carried
the weight of it.

A CERTAIN WOMAN wandered a desert
that smelled of salt, hoping
the trail of fragrance would lead her
toward oceans ripe for sailing.
But she found instead crystal pillars
shouldering the sky, crumbling
with the weight of it.

A CERTAIN STORY passes through roads
made of blood and home, sculpted from
wounds and words that sloped her back
into another mountain to clean and conquer.
She grew a garden
from the weight of it.

.

IN THE MARBLE I saw life
Engraved into an after-thought.
I wiped soil from sentiment
and asked her questions only
a ghost in my mind could answer.
I sat and listened
to the weight of it.

Joy

Remember
The thrum of engines pulsing
Forward, into seas
That pulled apart in me
The note of joy
From sorrowed songs
The taste of salt
From oceans fared
The pull of earth
From soaring skies.

Remember
The sound of metal scraping
Words from iron lungs
Rusted, bent, and crushed
Beneath the weight
Of time that hides
Between the threads
Of copper braids
Within the heart
With ashen breath.

Remember
The smoke of searing spells
Blinding eyes that seek
In me, the binal prayer
That built for me
A nest of twigs
And sang to me
A verse of flame
And heals in me
The joy of pain.

Lucidity

Phantom pain spins the yarn
Binding breath to tender bones
And stitches skin to leather wheels
Writing wills on streets unknown.
Unwind the roads that twist and turn
Open fields to empty sea.
Unravel self, pull the strings,
Unmake the thing inside of me.

Kill please the pulse that sings
To her the sounds of siren spheres
Stringing gravel into shores,
Unexplored but ventured near.
Ghosts of fear, wisps of flame,
Guide her back to light of day
In salted seams of sight unseen
Does she walk a waking dream.

Reality

One day, the devil told me,
Tomorrow is an illusion.
We are an immovable people
Pulled around an immovable sun.

I told myself to shut up,
And to wake up early to catch the first light.
And if it possessed me, to drive down the coast.
The sun is beautiful when it slips beyond the waves.

Ghosts in the forest

a woman's laughter
a man's scream
the screech of traffic
the shouts of drunkards.
An amorphous synchronization
of sound, burrowing into
Bones and buzzing like flies.

I find comfort in the white noise,
but he likes scuttle of animals,
the howl of the woods
the rustle of leaves.

The language of the forest seeps out
a quiet lull,
drifting us to sleep.

To you, Orlando

Orlando hides in waves of light
A speck of self in abstract mind
Bent and shaped by eons' spell
From scalding rock to icy hell.

Orlando writes his testament,
In clouds that paint the heavens gray
With dust that hides the burning suns
In signals sent from far away.

Orlando's inklings tuck away
In molten curves of infant cells
That aged and died in letters sent
Unopened on my windowsill.

Planets fade, to pearl, to dust
Celestial pathways break away
Orbits spin to slow decay,
Phantom traveler yet remains.

I throw myself into the space
Growing between your yesterdays.
I reflect myself upon a lake
With depths that drink your name away.

I hear your cry through weight of time
I chase the light I can't retain.
Orlando's skies now drift apart
And die in eyes unknown today.

In my bones, I carve your gaze,
Or try to, based on memory.
But even death has its grave
And so does the name

Orlando.

For Camille

I walk.

I know the rhythm of steps, one foot before another
Shoes broken in, leather-worn valleys rising
Where I'm going, where I've been.
I know the map of air, wind pushing me forward
And chafing trails into the crease of my palms.

One step, and then another,
Earth breaks beneath my boots, and my boots
Break beneath my feet. My path lies written
In lakes of red I've left behind, in a tongue
I will never speak, will never read.

Still, I walk.

My blood runs, and is caught by new thoughts
Finding forests in my flesh, and cutting my bones
Like trees, chipped away for a host not born of me.
I become smoke from a fire, a fossil in stone.
A fox in a den, sniffed out by the hound.

One step after another,
My limbs inherit my memory, and my feet learn
The ritual of reminiscence. My path lies written
In the shadows of tomorrow. The days we meet,
And the days we pass.

Still, I walk.

I follow the warmth of a flame,
It rages bright, a candle in a cave.
I chase it, an echo loudly dimming
To shades of orange, red, then black.
I know, one day, it will fade.

I follow it to strange lands, old and cold
I follow it to dark seas, miasmic pools.
Beyond a black horizon, it flickers and flies
And perches upon a faceless mountain
I once called eternity.

Still, I walk.

I follow to houses I leave unowned
I follow to cities made of bone
My hands outstretched to see the world
Veiled in horizons,only found
In last of light now left to me.

One foot after another
Unmanned vessel, buoyed on the lull of knees
Bending, heels burning, legs swaying. I became
Smoke from a fire, a fossil in stone. I knew
Nothing beyond the horizon.

Still, I walked.

My blood runs, a gentle river slacking
The thirst of new things growing within me.
Eyes bloom, black-eyed beneath their petals,
Blinking in wonder at prisms of grey
I once thought null and void.

One step after another,
A new world inherits my memory, and new lives lay
Last rites to remembrance. Their path lies written
In a communion for tomorrow. The days they meet,
And the days they pass.

Together, they walk.

Evolution

One day, you decide
You want someone like the ocean
And spend your days in the water
Chasing fish with your love.
And one day, you decide
You will teach your young
How to hide in the sea, and how
To hold a breath long enough
To hunt.
And one day it becomes tradition
To creep away from the shore
And find joy in the weight of foam
And in the rippling sunlight
Far from ancient depths.
And one day, a daughter decides
To stay where her heart lies,
The cool call
Of home.
And one day, a child will trade
The steady kiss of air
For the dark song of water
Older than memory.

Newton's Dream

I speak of beauty, of space between heavenly bodies
That holds the weight of travel, from here to there
I speak of lulling melodies, a celestial song
So sweet in its quiet, heavy in silence
Holding the weight of forever upon the tip of a tongue.
I speak of the fields growing skies unseen
Littered with salted soil, pockets of uncertain
Graves I call into.

I speak of beauty, of the still and quiet green captured
In the glass, for me to look and admire
Trees reaching out to blue hues kissing sunlight
Mountains breaking into the light of day
Rivers coursing through brown grass, silky and sweet.
I speak of beauty, within gaps of a pattern
The empty spaces in air, in sound,
Your laughter.

I speak of beauty, of a mother's steps remembered
Alongside riverbanks long ghost and gone.
Of little feet following, falling, fading;
Of her forgotten lullabies, echoes etched in winds
That pull sails across seas and clouds across skies,
And push the hair from your face
And dry the tears from your eyes.

I once believed my life was measured in seasons
Cycles of space to shape, from sound to silence
But a seed only brings one harvest, breaking
With the weight of life, and rising
Through the wheat, and through the grain.

How beautiful your pull, written into the fall
Of an apple.

BIO

Rosa Christina may be found somewhere in Southern California. Some say she has been spotted lurking the ruins of a forgotten Borders, but others know she lingers in her abode indefinitely. When she's not working her 9-5, Rosa enjoys reading fantasy novels, drawing tarot cards, and listening to horror podcasts while driving along the coast.